RED YELLOW GREEN

Insights on Dating for Teens

PARENT EDITION

CORTLAND JONES

JayMedia Publishing

Printed in the United States of America

First Printing, 2020

JayMedia Publishing

Laurel, MD 20708

ISBN 978-1-7334432-1-0

TABLE OF CONTENTS

FOREWORD

THE Teen Years…it's the season of parenting that most of us excitedly await as our children are on the cusp of adulthood. We've nurtured them from cradle to cars and everything in between, watched their wings mature and spread ready to fly, and beamed with pride as they created and achieved their personal, social, and academic goals. But transitioning to this season is usually accompanied with plenty of growing pains for our teens AND us! There's so much they desire to experience and accomplish that sometimes a derailment is inevitable.

Dating, for sure, is one of those areas! It is the gateway to the ultimate indicators of adulthood: love, marriage, and parenting. However, transitioning through the phases of a relationship is most successful with the engagement and support of people and helpful tools such as this book.

As our young people blossom into teens, it's not uncommon for them to seek and embrace greater independence. That means relying more on themselves and less on us; seeking information from external sources rather than from parental advice. Barriers are likely to form once we are out of the loop of influence in our teens' lives and as they re-evaluate their relationship with us as their parents. I have found that building solid communication eliminates potential barriers. It begins with simple actions such as assuring our teens that we are *"Team Them"*. Listening to their thoughts and hearts opens the door to understanding who they are - not who we want or expect them to be. It allows our teens to express their hopes, concerns, and fears safely without parental judgement. Establishing a code of respect is another way to boost their confidence in us. Demonstrating support in areas of their life important to them creates a connection beyond parental responsibility.

I was allowed to date at 16. While I had positive experiences, there were some scenarios I would rather forget. Those bad decisions reinforced my level of inexperience and taught me important life lessons. My mother's response to these moments taught me the importance of loyalty and trust. Regardless of my decisions and experiences, she was always supportive and my greatest confidant. I knew for certain she had my back to protect me and would **never** irresponsibly handle or expose me.

When I became a parent, emulating my mother's commitment to emotional security started for me as a parent from day one. As they have experienced life, good and disappointing, I have given them room to grow through youthful missteps and allow their recovery to occur in the privacy of our family not exposing them to the likes, dislikes, or judgements on Facebook. Cultivating a relational environment based on loyalty and trust has yielded huge dividends over the years and is still evidenced in my relationship with my teens today.

That practice of communication is now a regular occurrence especially since they have interests in dating. I have been awestruck and humbled by their comfort and courage to transparently share themselves with me, to seek my council, and to ask for honest feedback. It's been with ease that they share with me and that they extend me permission to share my dating experiences with them. While much of my experience occurred in a decade they can't relate to, my teens appreciate my candid memories that had a positive and/or negative impact on my life, even today! And the trust between us is priceless.

A benefit of developing solid communication skills is imparting your beliefs and values. It also allows parents to assist their teens in developing dating rules and responsibilities. As I recall my own dating years, I was a complete novice with limited direction and understanding of how dating really worked, understanding the "roles", and managing the expectations of my partner(s). Internet, Instagram, and other social media platforms were not available to follow "relationship goals". It was a wilderness exploration of figuring things out without the help of an advocate – someone who believes and supports my best interest – more importantly, someone who knew how to navigate dating better than me.

I recognize dating is inevitable, even anticipated for by my teens...whether I'm ready or not. Healthy dating skills are critical for normal, healthy development. Rather than releasing naïve, impetuous, or aloof youngsters, I want to ensure they are emotionally and mentally prepared for the experience with support, counsel, and positive strategies with an exit plan when necessary. For them to experience productive, non-heartbreaking encounters, they deserve time to practice under the supervision of their parents. That means accommodating movie dates, supporting teen social events, extending trust, and being confident with all the seeds we've planted during "real talk" sessions.

It's been a pleasure parenting my teens. The comfort of open dialog between us has afforded me and their dad the privilege of hearing their hearts, reasoning, and decision making particularly regarding dating. On any given day, young people are confronted with a variety of issues I never had to, or thought to consider. Dating today looks very little like what dating was when I was 16. Not only is the vocabulary different, the rules (or lack thereof) of engagement are equally different. I feel especially connected to them, as they trust me to share my perspective on a situation or set boundaries regarding a certain situation or input for a strategy needed to appropriately resolve a challenge. It is an adventure that's real-time for us but worth every moment knowing we are welcomed into our teens' dating season and serve as their personal dating consultants when they need us.

Felicia Jones Miller

PREFACE

STOP / CAUTION / PROCEED:

**Teen Dating Workbook
for Parents & Teens**

CONTENT from this Parent Edition of Red Yellow Green is written to help parents and their teens establish open lines of communication to discuss difficult topics like dating.

There are questions at the end of each reading for parents to reflect upon and answer. There are also questions to provide to your children for them to reflect upon.

Use the notes section to write down any thoughts or questions inspired from the content or to write down questions you would want to ask one another.

If you agree to read and discuss each of the books together, consider the following:

1. Identify a day and time best suited to read and discuss content

2. Agree on three to four simple rules you will hold each other accountable to follow when talking and sharing your thoughts/feelings

3. Identify movies or documentaries you could watch that support what you're learning as you talk about the book

4. What would be a great way to celebrate success with talking openly as you read the book and once you finish?

I hope this book will help enhance the communication around difficult topics and build rapport that will last long after you finish reading them.

INTRODUCTION

Start children off on the way they should go, and
even when they are old they will not turn from it.

- Proverbs 22:6 NIV

WHAT does God expect a parent to do when their child approaches them with an interest in dating?

This is actually the question I posed to my two adolescent children one day as we discussed the subject of dating. I explained to my children that I imagined God looking with amusement at me with the thought of wondering what I would say. I don't envision God wanting me to remain silent about it, to bury my head in the proverbial sand and ignore the opportunity, or suggest to my children that the topic is off limits for discussion. I imagine God is waiting to see whether I will respond in a way that allows my children to be informed, armed, and empowered with wisdom, insight, and information inspired from His word. I imagine He is waiting to see what I will say to help them navigate the reality of the world they are growing up in and one day will step into as young adults.

One of the main concerns of parents in having an open sincere dialogue about the subject of dating is the fear or concern children will see it as permission to engage in the desired activity simply because their parents would allow them to talk about it. Then there is the fear or concern that too much will be shared and may in some way damage and harm our children or as we would say as adults, 'scar them for life.' The emotion associated with the awkwardness, tension, and discomfort of having to address such a complex topic can make talking about dating a difficult conversation to have.

Every teen I have encountered, who initiated a conversation with me on the subject of dating, was encouraged to talk with their parents. Understanding not all parents are open to talking about the subject, I explained I could not discuss it without knowing if their parents would approve of them dating or even be open to discussing the subject. By the time a child transitions into an adolescent leaving elementary school, if not while in elementary school, they are becoming curious and experiencing physical, mental, and emotional changes that heighten their interest in peer relationships. Though parents may think not discussing dating may discourage their children from thinking about dating, it actually doesn't. It just discourages them from wanting to talk about it with their parents.

The most important tip I share with teens regarding talking with their parents about topics like dating is to make sure they are willing to address dating on an adult level since they are talking with an adult. They can't expect an adult to remain on their level of communication when addressing the topic. Likewise, a parent must learn to communicate with their child in a way that respects the child's thought process. An open-door policy won't work if children feel judged, ridiculed, criticized, or belittled for the way they think.

QUESTIONS FOR PARENTS TO CONSIDER

1. Why would it be important to discuss the topic of dating with your child?

2. What does it do for your relationship with your child to talk about difficult topics?

3. What does it do for your child to learn to talk about difficult topics with you?

4. What is the best way to talk about difficult topics with your child?

5. What do you need from your child to make talking about dating easier?

QUESTIONS FOR CHILDREN TO CONSIDER

1. What does it mean to talk on an adult level?

2. Why is it important to learn to talk with adults on an adult level about difficult topics?

3. Why would a parent hesitate or be uncomfortable to talk with their child about dating?

4. What would you need from your parents to make talking about dating easier?

5. Does talking about dating automatically mean you are ready to date? Why?

STOP / THINK / PROCEED WITH CAUTION

What are your thoughts?

_____

_____

_____

_____

_____

_____

_____

_____

_____

_____

_____

_____

_____

_____

_____

CHAPTER 1

STRATEGIC COMMUNICATION

*Fathers, do not exasperate your children; instead,
bring them up in the training and instruction
of the Lord.*

- Ephesians 6:4 NIV

UNDERSTANDING communication is a critical life skill vital to any healthy relationship. How important then is it to train our children to talk about difficult topics?

I have a fond memory that I often share with parents at the evening co-parenting seminar I facilitate for the National Family Resiliency Center. It involves my two children when they were ages six and seven. While eating together, my son, age six at the time, asked me where do babies come from? Unprepared to answer, I explained we would discuss that later. I knew it was important to provide an answer. I wanted to, but it was important to explain it in an age appropriate way and only answer the question that was asked. Later turned into two weeks, but I decided it was time. Listening to a radio show while driving home from work one day compelled me to take action and sit down with my children to answer the question.

I brought my son and my daughter with me over to the couch. With both of them comfortably nestled under each arm I took a deep breath. After exhaling, I calmly asked them a question that I figured their mom had discussed with them also. I began with my daughter since she was older and said, "Tell me what you know about sex." I paused awaiting her reply thinking she would say something that suggested her mom had already told her. My daughter then replied, "Well my friend said it's what her daddy does with another woman when he is angry with her mommy." Every time I share that story there is a HUGE outbreak of gasps, laughter, and "Whoooooa!" In that moment, I paused realizing my daughter was already talking about sex at age seven with a friend, mind you, who could not have been that much older than her. So my 'sex talk' with my children began when they were young. I also used a children's book that had an age appropriate illustration of an adult male and female in bed, under the covers, each on a separate side of the bed. I used it to explain how a baby is produced from having sex.

The emotions and thoughts you feel having to discuss sensitive topics like sex and dating are awkward and create tension, but I learned my daughter was already having the conversation at age seven. It taught me a valuable lesson that I can either begin to talk with my children and have them be properly informed or someone else is going to have that 'talk' with them; whether I do it or not. Consider these practical tips when seeking to communicate to your child or parent:

- Make eye contact
- Give undivided attention
- Turn off electronics
- Schedule talk time
- Find a quiet place
- Acknowledge feelings
- Listen
- Don't interrupt
- Don't talk child out of how they feel
- Get clarity
- Take a time out if talking leads to arguing
- Reschedule talk time when everyone is calm

QUESTIONS FOR PARENTS TO CONSIDER

1. Why is it important to not react when listening to your child talk?

2. Why should you not tell your child they shouldn't be feeling a certain way?

3. Active listening includes being able to identify with how the person is feeling and why this is important to them?

4. Indirectly, what is being communicated to a child when a parent does/does not listen?

5. What is a child learning when they can talk openly about difficult feelings, thoughts, and topics?

QUESTIONS FOR CHILDREN TO CONSIDER

1. Why may it be helpful to first write down what you want to talk about with your parents?

2. Why should you explain it's hard to talk about what YOU want to talk about and that it is important they listen without interrupting?

3. Why is it important to practice having conversations with your parents about difficult topics?

4. Why may it be a good idea to inform your parents you'd like to talk with them before the conversation takes place?

5. Why may it be helpful to your parents to explain how it makes you feel when you can/can't talk with them about your feelings and thoughts?

STOP / THINK / PROCEED WITH CAUTION

What are your thoughts?

_____

_____

_____

_____

_____

_____

_____

_____

_____

_____

_____

_____

_____

_____

RED YELLOW GREEN

CHAPTER 2

The Value of the Conversation: Connecting and Opening Lines of Communication

Honor your father and your mother, as the LORD
your God has commanded you, so that you may live
long and that it may go well with you in the land the
LORD your God is giving you.

- Deuteronomy 5:16 NIV

WHAT is the value of parents and teens being able to communicate with each other?

I remember picking my children up from their after-care karate program and after getting settled in the car beginning a conversation that went something like this: 'Hey, how was your day?' My children responded in unison, 'Fine.' I replied, 'What did you do today?' My children said, 'Nothing.' Immediately I recalled thinking I am doing the very thing parents are encouraged not to do; asking questions that could be answered with few words. So, I was ready the next time they got in the car. 'Hey, what was one thing you enjoyed doing today?' I asked. I began asking questions that motivated them to share interesting things about their day. They began raising their hand with enthusiasm when they got in the car to talk about their day. Then after the first question was asked, they would begin rattling off a list of events and things that occurred, which indicated they caught on to my routine of asking them about their day.

As my children grew in age, I made a conscious decision to go out to eat with each of them separately so they could have quality time with me apart from their sibling. I made going out to eat and talking about a family ritual and routine for us that continues to this day. At critical moments growing up as children, they each came forward to confide in me things that would have or could have caused them to get in trouble, and I consistently commended them for being courageous to speak up or admit when they were in the wrong. I have also had to apologize to my children for not always being emotionally present for them while they were growing up and I struggled with the outcome of separation and divorce. I have not been the perfect parent for my children.

An 'open door policy' is only effective when it allows our children to actually talk about what's on their hearts and minds. If we can talk to them about drugs, alcohol, and peer pressure, then we need to be able to talk about sex and dating. In fact, it's not the subject matter that is the focal point of why parents and teens need to be able to talk with each other. It's more about making connections that strengthen the relationship and keep the communication lines open in case of an emergency. I have recently explained to my children, as well as my students, that asking for help is a life skill. Even as an adult, life will put us in scenarios where we need to ask for help. It's important our children are comfortable and confident they can come to us to get help. Another reason our children need to learn how to have difficult conversations with us is so when they actually do begin dating, they need to have past experiences of expressing clarity of thought and managing difficult emotions during difficult conversations.

QUESTIONS FOR PARENTS TO CONSIDER

1. Why should parents talk with their children about dating even if they don't approve of their child dating?

2. What are your biggest concerns just thinking about the subject of dating and your child?

3. What are ways to communicate your concerns, fears, and feelings with your child besides verbally?

4. How can you create a family ritual and routine of talk time with your children?

5. If you have multiple children does the talk time have to be hours of time?

QUESTIONS FOR CHILDREN TO CONSIDER

1. Why should teens talk with their parents about dating even if you don't want to?

2. Why is it important to learn how to have difficult conversations with adults?

3. What are ways to communicate your thoughts, feelings, and concerns with your parents besides verbally?

4. Why is it important to understand a parent's concerns about the subject of dating and not disregard their concerns while talking with them?

5. While discussing the subject of dating, what do you think your parent is most concerned about, you or the subject of dating?

STOP / THINK / PROCEED WITH CAUTION

What are your thoughts?

_____

_____

_____

_____

_____

_____

_____

_____

_____

_____

_____

_____

_____

_____

_____

CHAPTER 3

A SUCCESSFUL LAUNCH

Children are a heritage from the LORD, offspring
a reward from him. Like arrows in the hands of a
warrior are children born in one's youth. Blessed is
the man whose quiver is full of them.

- Psalm 127:3-5a

WHY would talking with our children about dating be considered proactive parenting?

In a conversation with our son, I heard my son's mother refer to his transition into adulthood as a *launch* that triggered my recollection of the verse provided from Psalm 127. In a conversation with our daughter, I reminded her that our desire for her to wait, regarding dating, isn't about punishing her, but preparing her for her future. When the movie *Wonder Woman* was released, my children and I went to see it. I referred to the point in the movie where Diana was being trained to be who she would ultimately become, in conversation with my daughter, to reinforce the perspective of preparation for the future. Understanding this from seeing the movie herself, she could better accept the process of what her mother and I were seeking to do which was to prepare her for a successful launch into her life as a young adult.

A recurring memory as a parent influenced from movies, is the scene from *Father of the Bride* starring Steve Martin, where he is talking with his daughter who appears to be an elementary age child, but in actuality is a young adult. This scene often reminds me how difficult it is for parents to see our children growing up, because of the reality of the world they are growing into. As they grow, the less control we have over protecting them from that reality. Understanding this, I believe the best gift we can give our children is the ability to cope. Talking with our children about dating is a proactive way to help our children begin to cope with the real thoughts, feelings, and concerns they have about teen related issues. My main concern addressing the subject of dating with my children was the real social-emotional challenges and trauma encountered when teens get emotionally invested too soon and committed too seriously in dating relationships before they are able to handle them.

I've explained to my children everything they learn can't be learned from the couch. I've also mentioned wisdom does not always have to come from making poor decisions and mistakes. Wisdom can help me not make mistakes and poor decisions, that don't require hardship in order to understand a decision shouldn't be made. Talking with our children about dating allows us opportunity to address topics like:

- decision making
- problem solving
- managing thoughts and emotions
- Self-discipline
- time management
- goal setting
- dealing with peer pressure
- identifying toxic behavior in others
- integrity, and so much more.

One of my proudest moments as a parent was hearing my daughter communicate ending a relationship at the end of her junior year. It was because she knew he was transitioning into college, and didn't see the need to hang onto a relationship her then boyfriend was trying to encourage her to keep. It was a lesson of not prioritizing short-term goals, like dating, over life goals that I had encouraged my children to be mindful of whether they were dating or not.

QUESTIONS FOR PARENTS TO CONSIDER

1. How can talking about dating help a child think about and prepare for the future?

2. Is it possible that talking openly about dating with your child can actually cause them to delay being seriously committed and invested in wanting to date?

3. Does the talk about dating mean our children won't make mistakes and demonstrate poor decision making?

4. Whether children date or not, why is it important to teach them to talk about their thoughts and feelings?

5. Besides you and books, what other resources are available to you to address difficult topics like dating with your child?

QUESTIONS FOR CHILDREN TO CONSIDER

1. What does it mean to not prioritize short term goals like dating, over life goals like graduating from high school, going to college, buying a house, etc.?

2. Why is it important to learn to prioritize goals, short term and long term?

3. What are ways to learn how to express and manage your thoughts and feelings?

4. Why should a teenager delay dating if they struggle with managing their emotions, schoolwork, and handling stressful circumstances?

5. Why should a teenager not date if their parents disapprove of it?

STOP / THINK / PROCEED WITH CAUTION

What are your thoughts?

_____

_____

_____

_____

_____

_____

_____

_____

_____

_____

_____

_____

_____

_____

CHAPTER 4

INSTILLING A HEALTHY SENSE OF SELF IN OUR CHILDREN SELF-ESTEEM

*Therefore encourage one another and build each
other up, just as in fact you are doing.*

- 1 Thessalonians 5:11 NIV

DO you understand what self-esteem is?

Having the opportunity to teach writing enrichment the past two school years, has afforded me the opportunity to share with my students my understanding of self-esteem. Taking each word separately, I explained that self is in reference to them as an individual; and the word esteem means to honor, hold in high regard, or place great value on something. When put together, I understand the word self-esteem to mean what a person does to honor themselves, hold themselves in high regard, and place great value upon self. The practical way I have conveyed this to youth is to encourage them to learn to be consistent positive contributors to self, home, school, and community.

I reinforce this concept by explaining to them to do three things:

1. Identify and participate in activities of interest to them (hobbies) unrelated to school, television, video games, and excessive cell phone use

2. Work hard at school

3. Identify healthy effective ways of expressing their thoughts and feelings (journaling)

True self-esteem is not what someone says to make me feel good about myself. I explained to my students that it is encouragement or affirmation. Our children need to be taught how to say and do things that make them feel good about themselves, and not become dependent on what others say to make them feel good about who they are. This is important because they are growing up into a world where they will be faced with negativity and challenging circumstances. Learning how to affirm themselves, cope with negative circumstances, people, and feelings, while also learning to encourage themselves and affirm their self-worth, are critical life skills they need to possess. The encouragement and affirmation we provide for our children as they grow is part of instilling a healthy sense of self into them; that allows them to grow up with a healthy self-concept.

Self-concept is the idea or concept a person has of themselves and how they see themselves in an environment. A child can feel really good about who they are at home where they are loved, accepted, and supported, but not feel so great at school where they may be struggling with math, dealing with the school bully, or finding it difficult to make new friends. The best thing to understand about self-concept is that it is always evolving, so who your child is today, even if they're struggling, does not mean they will struggle forever. Encouraging, challenging, and leaving room for our children to grow, think, problem solve, and communicate, are simple ways of developing a healthy self-concept. Helping our children in the development of a healthy self-concept, and teaching them to build their self-esteem, begins with identifying what the self-concept consists of, and thinking of practical ways to engage children in their personal growth and development. Self-concept consists of the following:

- Self-awareness
- Self-image
- Self-confidence
- Self-discipline
- Self-esteem
- Self-fulfillment

QUESTIONS FOR PARENTS TO CONSIDER

1. What are practical ways, at home, you can affirm who your child is, verbally and non-verbally?

2. Why is it important for your child to hear you express what you appreciate about them?

3. How would a child benefit from a proactive parent invested in their interests?

4. How do rules, expectations, consequences, and letting children talk out loud about how to solve problems at school, help them in their self-concept development?

QUESTIONS FOR CHILDREN TO CONSIDER

1. What are your strengths, things you are good at, activities unrelated to school that you enjoy, that don't include watching television, playing video games, talking on the phone?

2. What ideas do you have about future career interests or life after high school?

3. What was one thing you accomplished recently that was difficult at first, and how did that make you feel?

4. Why do you think it is important to have a healthy sense of self before getting involved in dating relationships?

STOP / THINK / PROCEED WITH CAUTION

What are your thoughts?

_____

_____

_____

_____

_____

_____

_____

_____

_____

_____

_____

_____

_____

_____

CHAPTER 5

PRIORITIZING WHAT MATTERS MOST

*Be very careful, then, how you live—not as unwise
but as wise, making the most of every opportunity,
because the days are evil. Therefore do not be foolish, but understand what the Lord's will is.*

- Ephesians 5:15-17 NIV

HOW do you teach your child to be passionate, hungry, or demonstrate initiative?

To this day, I still cringe as I reflect on listening to middle school children explain to me their desire to date; or the fact they had already been involved in dating relationships, some as long as two years in length. I recall a student on the high school level who visited my office wanting to talk to me, upset with her mom for demanding she end her relationship with her boyfriend or she would no longer be living at home. In my mind, at the time, I couldn't understand why a child would opt for a relationship with another teenager over being at home. I remember repeatedly asking the girl why she would choose her boyfriend over living at home. Initially, she kind of understood that I was trying to help her separate the emotion of what she was feeling, from the reality of what she was expressing and strongly considering doing. I am also reminded of the student who came to me expressing her understanding, from our previous conversations, the need to let go of an unhealthy relationship and move on, but asking for help, pleading to understand how to do it.

This reminds me of a simple conversation I had with my two children one day while we were in the car. Speaking of dating, I explained to them they could either be in disagreement with us as their parents, and have to look for a place to live and provide for themselves; or be in disagreement with us on the subject of dating but still enjoy a roof over their heads, food to eat, and the comfort of being taken care of. I said this after explaining to them the story, involving the girl who allowed her emotions to let her consider leaving home over a fight with her mom about her boyfriend. I explained early on to both of my children that having the permission to date meant, prior to dating, learning to communicate with their parents and making sure they kept their attitudes in check, if they desired to have our approval to date. Talking about the subject of dating, and reading books on the subject, were a requirement before they were allowed to date. Establishing open lines of communication was also required.

I cringed at hearing middle school students inquire or talk about being involved in dating relationships, because most teenagers have yet to learn fully about whom they are and deal effectively with managing their emotions, before being involved in committed relationships. I explained this to my son that emotions are what drive most teen decision making. Emotions become intensified when you add the challenges associated with dating on top of that. Proactive parenting involves teaching our children to invest the energy they desire to put into dating, into being/doing their best academically, emotionally, and socially.

QUESTIONS FOR PARENTS TO CONSIDER

1. What is a benefit to setting ground rules about difficult subjects like dating, driving, parties, etc. before your children engage in these activities?

2. How does expressing gratitude or appreciation for the consistent positive things your child does help them?

3. Why is learning to listen, without reacting, a helpful tip for parents talking with their teens?

4. What are practical ways to reinforce helping your child become more independent, and to be a positive contributor at home?

QUESTIONS FOR CHILDREN TO CONSIDER

1. What do you do when you struggle with how you feel?

2. Why would doing chores and being a positive contributor at home be beneficial?

3. Why is it important to not always be told what to do by your parents?

4. If children are struggling with school, chores, and managing themselves, are they actually ready for the commitment and responsibility of being in a relationship?

STOP / THINK / PROCEED WITH CAUTION

What are your thoughts?

_____

_____

_____

_____

_____

_____

_____

_____

_____

_____

_____

_____

_____

_____

_____

_____

CHAPTER 6

LOVE

*Instead, speaking the truth in love, we will grow to
become in every respect the mature body of him who
is the head, that is, Christ'*

- Ephesians 4:15 NIV

HOW does talking about dating demonstrate love to our
children?

When I began my initial talks with my two children,
I acknowledged to them it would be a difficult conversation to have. The emotion that is felt and creeps into
the conversation while discussing dating, is what actually
makes talking about it difficult. In the times I had talked
with teens on the subject of dating, I always maintained
the position that teens would need to elevate their conversation and understanding of dating on the level of their
adult parents, and not just think about the subject matter
from their perspective. In the same way, parents would

need to learn to engage their teenage children in conversation and understanding on their level too. This is to avoid a communication style that sounds like we are talking down, at, or to our children in a manner that makes it difficult to keep the communication lines open. It is a conversation that seeks to understand and be understood. It should be conducted with patience, gentleness, compassion, and sincerity.

A recent conversation with my son prompted me to ask him about his teen years from ages 12 to 17. I asked him how often he had heard the subject of dating in a sermon from the pulpit, or in a lesson led by his youth pastor. He responded, within that five-year time span it had not been very often. My reply to him reinforced my understanding that many teens are involved in the activity of dating with or without their parents' approval and supported the importance of engaging them in dialogue on the subject. My motivation to talk with my children, as I explained to my daughter, was so they could be informed about what they would eventually be engaging in when they were on their own as young adults. An informed child is an empowered child, and children are less likely to engage in risky behaviors when they are informed about the dangers associated with them. As difficult and awkward as having the conversation can be, I sincerely believe our children want us to have the conversation with them, because they have a lot of thoughts, and see a lot of things happening around them. It would reduce the anxiety felt from that reality by making them feel informed and affirmed.

Within that five-year window, the ages between 12 and 17, both of my children have come forward to admit mistakes and poor decisions they made and to confess moments where they fell short of what was expected of them. In their prodigal moments, however, I rejoice in knowing they, like the prodigal son, felt they could return home and admit their need for forgiveness, support, and help. While they were teens, the story of the prodigal son was a subject we discussed often. I believe it aided in estab-lishing open lines of communication and created the space and opportunity for them to return to their parents during their prodigal moments. Let love guide you in establishing open lines of communication.

QUESTIONS FOR PARENTS TO CONSIDER

1. Why would admitting to your child that having a conversation about a particular subject would be difficult, be helpful to your child?

2. Do you agree that our children need to learn how to communicate during stressful, tense situations?

3. Do you think talking with your children about difficult topics aids them in learning how to communicate in stressful moments?

4. What do you think is the most important factor in establishing open lines of communication?

QUESTIONS FOR CHILDREN TO CONSIDER

1. What is your understanding of love?

2. What does it mean to love yourself?

3. Why would learning to love yourself before you begin dating be important?

4. Do you see your parents not approving of you dating as an act of love or a punishment?

STOP / THINK / PROCEED WITH CAUTION

What are your thoughts?

_____

_____

_____

_____

_____

_____

_____

_____

_____

_____

_____

_____

_____

_____

_____

FAMILY

Children, obey your parents in the Lord,
for this is right.

- Ephesians 6:1 NIV

WHY is it important for parents to talk on the level of their teens and not down to them or at them?

As a teenager, the extent of my talking about dating and sex involved my mom entering my room to hand me a book and walking out. Though I was the last of four children a lot of my childhood felt like being an only child. My parent's divorce at the time I was born left me without a strong foundation from which to have a successful transition into adulthood. In regard to parental involvement, my children's mother and I worked hard to provide for our children, despite getting divorced when our children were toddlers. I explained to my children that a lot of what I learned about relationships and transitioning into

---

FAMILY   45 adulthood was learned through trial and error. This motivated my desire to create an environment where open lines of communication would be established, so my children would feel comfortable talking to me, especially in times of crisis.

Establishing family rituals and routines that create an environment where our children feel safe, secure, loved, valued and accepted, goes a long way in fostering open lines of communication. One way I did this was to institute a 'hug break' with my children. At any random moment I would yell out, "Hug Break!" We would then stop and give each other huge hugs. We also had consistent times where we played board games as a family or went out to eat and talk. Reading children's books, devotional books, and discussing the content of the books was something I did with my children while they were young also. I loved watching movies too, so we shopped for movies they would be interested in watching. I would watch the Veggie Tales movies with them, and we would laugh and enjoy the content of those animated cartoons, that provided great moral lessons and addressed child related issues at an age appropriate level.

I recall a conversation I had with a friend who had concerns about her two children's welfare, while the family was going through separation and divorce. We talked about the importance of just checking in with our children to see how things are going and making sure everything was okay with them. My friend mentioned to me a difficult encounter where she tried checking in with the younger of her two children, who was more reserved and quieter in comparison with her older sister. I explained how sometimes the routine of life doesn't always help a child feel there is 'time' to talk. My friend later explained that her daughter alluded to the fact that when they were on vacation, she felt more relaxed and willing to open up, than when they were in their routine at home. In a conversation with my son, I mentioned how, as parents, we teach our children certain things, but sometimes forget to teach them to talk about how they feel.

QUESTIONS FOR PARENTS TO CONSIDER

1. What is a ritual or routine you've established that creates an opportunity to talk?

2. Why are these rituals and routines important?

3. Do you schedule opportunities to rest from the routine of the week?

4. Why is rest from the routine of the week important to include as a ritual?

QUESTIONS FOR CHILDREN TO CONSIDER

1. What is an activity you enjoy doing with/as a family?

2. What are ways to communicate with your parents other than talking?

3. Why is it good to read books together with your parents and discuss them, even as a teen?

4. What are some challenges or possible negative outcomes of dating without parent approval, knowledge, or adult input?

STOP / THINK / PROCEED WITH CAUTION

What are your thoughts?

_____

_____

_____

_____

_____

_____

_____

_____

_____

_____

_____

_____

_____

_____

_____

CHAPTER 8

FRIENDSHIP

The righteous choose their friends carefully.

- Proverbs 12:26a

WHY would it be important to talk with our teens about the characteristics of a good friend?

One thing I learned, while working with middle school aged teens outside of the classroom, was their need to understand who a friend was and how to establish healthy boundaries in order to minimize the amount of negativity caused by toxic relationships. In my role as the Peer Mediation Coordinator at the middle and high school level, I was responsible for training students to help their peers talk out conflicts they encountered. Those conflicts ranged from misunderstandings and disagreements, to rumors, gossip, and threats. At the middle school level, a majority of the conflicts involved, 'he said, she said,' and related to students who thought they were confiding in a friend. That friend would then relay what they had received to someone they considered a trustworthy friend, and eventually what was shared would be misconstrued or spread like wildfire or both. When I first took this position in 2001-2002, one of the administrators provided me some helpful advice about teens and the subject of friendship and asked me to teach the students about friendship. As I began to listen to the types of conflicts the students were having, I understood how timely and helpful the advice was while helping the students learn more about friendship. This prompted me to reflect on why friendship was such a challenging issue for students at the middle school level. Through reflection, I realized most students come out of the elementary school community thinking everyone is their friend, because that's the word we use to identify the people we know or get along with. You don't hear elementary students identifying their peers as associates or making a distinction between friends and associates. So, I began to help students identify the qualities of a real friend to avoid confiding in people who were not demonstrating those qualities. Having these types of conversations with their parents, instead of learning important life skills through trial and error, will help them better navigate the challenges of transitioning from adolescence to an adult.

I had students, at the high school level, still struggling with the 'healthy boundaries' concept of what to share and what to keep confidential. Through talks, one student learned the importance of ending unhealthy dating relationships, and wanted to know how to move forward once the relationship ended. Benefits of establishing open lines of communication with your children include listening to your children talk about these real-world challenges, and talking through with them healthy, effective ways to solve problems. This enhances their decision making with teen related issues. This is what teaching our children how to cope with the challenges they face involves. This also reinforces the critical life skill of learning to ask for help. I have explained to my children and students that this is important during the transition into adulthood. Talking reinforces and encourages asking for help.

QUESTIONS FOR PARENTS TO CONSIDER

1. Why is it important to not always tell our children what to do in problem solving?

2. How do children benefit from talking out their problems with their parents?

3. What resources are available for parents to aid them when talking about teen related topics?

4. How does open communication with your child help them with peer relationships?

QUESTIONS FOR CHILDREN TO CONSIDER

1. Is there a difference between having friends of the opposite sex and dating them without sex in the relationship? Explain.

2. What does it mean to be cautious or careful in friendship and establish healthy boundaries?

3. What are some good tips for ending a friendship or dating relationship when you're no longer interested in being in it?

4. Why is it important to learn how to have healthy boundaries and end relationships that aren't healthy?

STOP / THINK / PROCEED WITH CAUTION

What are your thoughts?

_____

_____

_____

_____

_____

_____

_____

_____

_____

_____

_____

_____

_____

_____

CHAPTER 9

FAITH

*Lord, you alone are my portion and my cup; you
make my lot secure. The boundary lines have fallen
for me in pleasant places; surely I have
a delightful inheritance.*

- Psalm 16:5-6 NIV

HOW do parents help their children develop and cultivate a faith relationship with God?

It is both natural and normal for teens to seek out and have desire for peer relationships during their adolescent years. It is part of normal growth and development for them during that time. The way I explained it to my children is that everything that we need to become an adult is already within us, including the desire for companionship, marriage, children, etc. Along with the 'raging hormones' normally associated with the adolescent child are the thoughts, desires, and passion for things associated with relationships outside of their parents, siblings, and family. As much as we think they shouldn't be thinking about sex, dating, and relationships, it doesn't change the fact that they are. What they need is guidance and support to help them develop the critical thinking, decision making, and problem-solving skills needed to manage all of the information they are receiving from the world around them. This part of their growth isn't fully developed until they are in their mid-twenties, so teenagers will consistently be driven by their thoughts and emotions more than logic, reason, and rational thinking. To help them develop critical thinking, decision making, and problem-solving skills requires patience and open dialogue, allowing them to process information and discuss appropriate ways of solving problems.

I have found that engaging my children in Bible studies and discussing passages of scripture is helpful in a practice I call 'strategic communication.' Strategic communication is deliberate, intentional conversation, engaging the listener in processing information, to identify and understand how they process information, and where their current level of understanding is. Simply put I would ask questions. In order to understand what our children are thinking we have to take time to listen to them talk about what's on their mind. Deuteronomy 6:6-7 reinforces to parents God's expectation of having His word in our hearts and impressing it upon our children. *'These commandments that I give you today are to be on your hearts. Impress them on your children. Talk about them when you sit at home and when you walk along the road, when you lie down and when you get up.' - Deuteronomy 6:6-7 NIV.* The Bible is the wisdom of God, inspired from the mind of God, on the way He desires for His people to live on the Earth. This passage in Deuteronomy reveals God's expectation that we talk with our children as often and as much as possible, in every way imaginable, in any setting.

Some practical ways I encouraged my children to develop a faith relationship with God included:

- Watching Veggie Tales animated videos together
- Reading children's book - versions of stories from the Bible
- Reading aloud and discussing Bible verses and stories together
- Having them write down thoughts of what they read in the Bible to discuss
- Encouraging time to pray, journal, and read the Bible independently

QUESTIONS FOR PARENTS TO CONSIDER

1. Would you rather your children learn about dating from you or their peers?

2. Why would taking your child to church not be enough to encourage a faith relationship with God?

3. What practical activities involve having a faith relationship with God?

4. How does the initiative of helping your child develop a faith relationship with God express love to God and your child?

QUESTIONS FOR CHILDREN TO CONSIDER

1. What do you think God's view is about dating as a teen?

2. What would be His expectations?

3. How much energy do you currently put into developing a faith relationship with God compared to the energy you put into developing a dating relationship?

4. Why would it be important to establish a faith relationship with God before dating?

STOP / THINK / PROCEED WITH CAUTION

What are your thoughts?

_____

_____

_____

_____

_____

_____

_____

_____

_____

_____

_____

_____

_____

_____

_____

_____

_____

CHAPTER 10

LIFE GOALS

*All hard work brings a profit, but mere talk
leads only to poverty.*

- Proverbs 14:23 NIV

HOW do we, as parents, teach our children to be hungry, passionate, and driven?

During a difficult season of my son's life I simply communicated to him, "When you wanted something to eat as a child you could go to the refrigerator to get food. When you wanted a toy, I could go to the store to get you Legos. I can't go get you, playing on the basketball team, graduating from high school, going to college, or your future career. Those are things you must learn how to go after and learn to get yourself." Raising teenagers is not easy. They are like two-year-old toddlers with the desire to do things their own way, demonstrate independence, but have an extended vocabulary to express more than "No,"

"Mine," or "Let me do it." That two-year-old toddler, who wanted to have things their way, has not forgotten about that natural inclination to want to have things their way. Now that they are older, bigger, and realize we have less control over their actions, they exercise that independence more. Whether we call it rebellion or a demonstration of their independence doesn't change the reality that they are seeking to display more autonomy in their decision making. Proactive parenting supports this, because we are actually raising our children to be independent of us, so they can learn to live on their own, and become happy, healthy, positive contributors at home, at school, and in the community, as they transition into adulthood.

With my children, I simply reiterated my desire that they learn to not prioritize short term goals, like the desire to date, over long term 'life goals,' like graduating from high school, college, and pursuing their career. I asked them whether simply having a boyfriend or girlfriend would help them graduate from high school or college or secure their dream job? In preparing for college, did they think one of the entry questions would include how many dating relationships they had in high school? At times they would express their concerns and feelings that our perspective of the topic was overblown. I would reiterate to them that God used words like death, destruction, poverty, and ruin to emphasize the importance of understanding the impact of not applying wisdom to decision making, critical thinking, and problem solving. Studies actually indicate a child is less likely to engage in risky behavior consistently, when they have ongoing parent-child conversations in comparison to being left to themselves.

Some practical strategies I employed to guide my children in learning to set goals and be intentional about following through included:

- Talking about future career interests
- Researching colleges of interest related to career interests
- Introducing them to people in the field of their career interests
- Attending college tours
- Discussing graduation requirements related to career interests
- Involving them with mentors and workshops
- Journaling and writing down their goals
- Creating a vision board of their goals
- Talking with them about time-management
- Using Google calendar

QUESTIONS FOR PARENTS TO CONSIDER

1. Why would it be helpful to talk with your child about their future career interests?

2. What is the conflict of trying to talk them out of their career interests?

3. What is the conflict of choosing their career path for them or telling them which way to go?

4. What are ways to help them understand your concerns about a particular career path without trying to talk them out of it?

QUESTIONS FOR CHILDREN TO CONSIDER

1. Why should dating not be prioritized over life goals?

2. As a teen, what is the complication and conflict of making dating the priority, or primary focus, of your life?

3. What are some important tips to make life goals a priority over dating?

4. Why is it important to begin thinking about your future career interests/path as a teen?

STOP / THINK / PROCEED WITH CAUTION

What are your thoughts?

_____

_____

_____

_____

_____

_____

_____

_____

_____

_____

_____

_____

_____

_____

_____

_____

CHAPTER 11

ADULTHOOD: MANHOOD

When I was a child, I talked like a child, I thought like a child, I reasoned like a child. When I became a man, I put the ways of childhood behind me.

- 1 Corinthians 13:11 NIV

WHAT are three important qualities a male child needs transitioning into adulthood?

In conversation with my son about what being a man meant to him, he responded by stating a man needs to be wise, strong, and self-controlled. I liked his response and it allowed me to see where his mind was on the subject. It gave me insight of what it meant to him and about the man he would transition into as an adult. Every now and then we would have a conversation about what being a man meant to him related to these three attributes, and I would ask how he might deal with challenges he faced, based on those qualities. I wanted to use the standard he provided as a basis to reinforce to him how he should think critically, make decisions, and solve problems while consistently displaying wisdom, strength, and self-control. Despite the reality of being a teenager, experiencing growing pains as all teens do, and sometimes falling short and not following through with tasks he is required to do, I am proud of who he is and who he is becoming.

Of the three attributes mentioned; wisdom, self-control, and strength, the one that is most critical to me in a teen's growth and development would be wisdom. It is equally important that my children display what generations past referred to as 'common sense,' or as I would say, being as intelligent dealing with life as you are academically. This creates a responsibility and challenge for me as a parent to make sure I am actively involved in engaging my son and daughter in conversations about teen related issues. It is important to:

1. Get an understanding of how they think about the things I am concerned about,

2. Identify strategic ways and means by which to have conversations with them that minimizes the amount of times they shut down and refuse to engage in open dialogue. Timing becomes a critical factor in this equation of strategic communication

to ensure we each are in a space and place that facilitates comfort, calmness, and openness.

As a parent, I have to recognize when my emotions are interfering with me and my child's ability to communicate with each other. Emotion is the major factor that makes communication difficult to have. How I am feeling at the time my child is communicating interferes with:

1. My ability to listen carefully

2. My ability to hear what's not being said

3. My ability to empathize with what is being felt in what is being said

4. My ability to remain objective and consider my child's perspective without being ready to pounce because they've articulated something that I don't agree with

5. The ability to control my emotions so they do not escalate when things are said that will only make communicating in the future that much more difficult. It is important that males learn to communicate and verbalize their thoughts and feelings.

QUESTIONS FOR PARENTS TO CONSIDER

1. What are some important specific things you want your son to know about dating?

2. How can a mother be helpful in talking with their son about dating?

3. Is the subject of manhood specifically about masculinity or something more?

4. Why is it important for male children to learn to communicate and express their thoughts and feelings?

QUESTIONS FOR CHILDREN TO CONSIDER

1. On a scale of 1-4, how would you rate your desire / ability to communicate thoughts and feelings consistently? **1** rather stay quiet, **2** hesitant, **3** open to talking, and **4** very confident

2. If your answer to question #1 is less than 3, what do you think the reason is?

3. Why do you think it would be helpful to learn to communicate openly, especially in a dating relationship?

4. What is one thing that concerns you when talking with your parents, one thing you'd like them to do when talking, or what do your parents do to make it helpful to talk with them?

STOP / THINK / PROCEED WITH CAUTION

What are your thoughts?

CHAPTER 12

ADULTHOOD: WOMANHOOD

Do not give dogs what is sacred; do not throw your pearls to pigs. If you do, they may trample them under their feet, and turn and tear you to pieces.

- Matthew 7:6 NIV

HOW do we teach our female child to have a healthy self-worth and high self-esteem?

In a conversation with my daughter, I shared insight I received from a conversation about self-esteem. I explained it was important that a distinction is made in how she carried herself as a young adult female. I compared it to business and how she should distinguish between being a lemonade stand, a nonprofit, and a business firm. Similar to the verse Matthew 7:6, the message is about understanding your self-worth enough to not allow yourself to be treated like pearls being trampled, by someone who does not value or appreciate who you are. Acting like a 'lemonade stand' involves giving yourself away to any passer-by thinking the attention alone is what validates your self-worth. A female who acts as a lemonade stand only sees their value in how often they are taken by someone or in a relationship with someone, regardless of the quality of the relationship. A 'lemonade stand' is more focused on the quantity of pursuers who give them attention. Because *attention* is the goal of validating their self-worth, a female who is a lemonade stand, only sees her self-worth in how often she can give herself away to those who are willing to take what she offers.

A female who distinguishes herself as a nonprofit see dating relationships with males as a project, they are responsible for enhancing or improving, without any necessary true commitment or consistent initiative from the male. A female nonprofit operates believing they can fix or improve the person they are dating. They think the person they are dating will change simply because they are in a relationship with them. The female nonprofit begins to invest their time and resources into the relationship giving, 110% of themselves, despite apparent evidence the person they're dating is not consistently putting in effort to change, evolve, and grow within the relationship. They are reaping ALL the benefits of the female's resources without exerting themselves in any meaningful, tangible way or reciprocating benefits to the female nonprofit. When the relationship ends, the female nonprofit is depleted, exhausted of resources, and unable to build themselves back up from having spent so much wasted effort hoping the person would change.

A female who distinguishes herself as a business firm understands her own value and worth. She is not driven by emotion or low self-esteem regarding dating. She is genuinely satisfied being single and consistently unbothered by feelings of loneliness, because she understands that a dating relationship does not solve that problem. She knows she can be dating and still feel lonely. Dating is an extended privilege and is invited only by interest, upon review of the male applicant. Time is taken to determine whether the male applicant is qualified to fill the position, based upon the high standards that have been previously determined as requirement by the "business firm". A female distinguished as a business firm has a 'no pearl trampling policy' and has trained herself to identify quickly applicants that are not qualified to even apply for the position.

QUESTIONS FOR PARENTS TO CONSIDER

1. Beyond the words of affirmation that we speak to our children, how do we help them 'feel' worthy and valuable?

2. Why is it important to explain why sex won't improve or make a relationship last?

3. What are 3 important qualities or character traits important for a female child to display transitioning into adulthood?

4. *The wise woman builds her house, but with her own hands a foolish one tears hers down.' - Proverbs 14:1* What does this verse mean and how is it related to dating?

QUESTIONS FOR CHILDREN TO CONSIDER

1. Why is it important to learn how to encourage and affirm yourself to make you feel good about who you are?

2. What is one behavior to avoid so that you do not act like a lemonade stand or nonprofit?

3. What is one behavior to demonstrate being like a business firm?

4. Why is it important to understand who you are before getting involved in serious committed relationships?

STOP / THINK / PROCEED WITH CAUTION

What are your thoughts?

_____

_____

_____

_____

_____

_____

_____

_____

_____

_____

_____

_____

_____

_____

_____

_____

CHAPTER 13

PERSPECTIVE: ADULT/YOUTH

After three days they found him in the temple courts,
sitting among the teachers, listening to them and
asking them questions. Everyone who heard him was
amazed at his understanding and his answers.

- Luke 2:46-47 NIV

WHAT are ways or means to talk with our teens about dating other than using our words?

Every time I engaged in conversation about teens talking with their parents, I would use the example of "going to the movies." I would explain to teens that when they ask their parents for permission to go to the movies with a 'friend,' the word movies would set off an alarm and cascade thoughts associated with sex in the mind of a parent. I would remind teens that whether it was their desire or not, it wouldn't change the fact that parents would have that perspective. With this understanding in mind, I would remind teens the importance of learning to talk about subjects like going to the movies, dating, etc. from the perspective of an adult. I would remind them that if their desire is to have their parents listen to them and receive approval from them to date, go to the mall, movies, etc., they need to be able to understand the real concerns that parents have. Teens don't always think about or simply are unaware of some of the harsh realities in the world around them. I believe this type of communication helps teenagers develop the wisdom necessary to navigate the world they are growing up in without having to always learn from their mistakes. As I've explained to my own two children, wisdom doesn't always have to be learned from making mistakes. Wisdom can help us avoid making mistakes that aren't necessary. Wisdom helps us to understand that something shouldn't be done.

Luke 2:46-47 always reinforced to me the value of youth and adults having open lines of communication when addressing teen related issues. The verse also reinforces why it's important for youth to learn to talk on an adult level. Likewise, closer inspection of the verses reveals that the adults allowed Jesus to express his thoughts and views on the various topics. They talked about being amazed at his responses. The emphasis is on the adults allowing him room and opportunity to express himself. A teenager, no matter how intelligent or smart they are, is limited in what they know due to their shorter life experience.

The true purpose of talking with our children and establishing open lines of communication is to simply gauge and have an understanding of what they know in regards to our concerns as adults. Not to prove what they don't know, chastise them for being unaware or ignorant of a particular topic, or expect them to know more than what they do. As parents, our focus should be on the days when our children are adults, on their own, and may be in a time of need, in a crisis, or experiencing an emergency and need to know what to do. We want our children to feel that home is still a place they can return to and receive help. Along with being a parent, as they transition into adulthood, we become consultants for our children, continuing to help them grow in wisdom, as they seek us out for advice. They need our input to fortify their critical thinking skills, decision making, and problem solving.

QUESTIONS FOR PARENTS TO CONSIDER

1. What is one challenge when listening to a teen talk about any particular topic?

2. What is one positive quality your child demonstrates when you do talk?

3. Why is it helpful to praise your child after a successful conversation or express appreciation for them being willing to listen/talk?

4. Why is it good to acknowledge or apologize for not handling a conversation well?

QUESTIONS FOR CHILDREN TO CONSIDER

1. Why is it important to talk about the specific concerns your parents have about dating whether you think it could happen or not?

2. Besides sex, what are some real legitimate concerns about dating as a teenager?

3. Besides holding hands, what is involved in a dating relationship as a teenager?

4. What are warning signs of being in an unhealthy teen dating relationship?

STOP / THINK / PROCEED WITH CAUTION

What are your thoughts?

_____

_____

_____

_____

_____

_____

_____

_____

_____

_____

_____

_____

_____

_____

_____

_____

CHAPTER 14

WISDOM

Know also that wisdom is like honey for you: If you find it, there is a future hope for you and your hope will not be cut off.

- Proverbs 24:14 NIV

WHY would reading and discussing books together, that are related to teen topics, be beneficial to your teenager?

I remember a proud parent moment while talking with my daughter over lunch. She told me she had to explain to her former boyfriend the relationship was ending because he would be transitioning to college and she would still be in her senior year in high school. Even though he still desired to continue the relationship, she remained firm in her position to end the relationship. I expressed how proud I was of her for making a wise decision and having the foresight to choose to end the relationship. It would spare her the unnecessary emotion and drama of trying to maintain a relationship with someone who would not be close in proximity. She would be spared all of the drama associated with wondering what is or isn't happening with him on campus while she's still in high school. I also commended her for not allowing him to convince her to stay in the relationship, when it was her desire to end it.

I explained to my children that all the lessons of life they would need to learn would not be learned from the couch. Talking about dating and actually experiencing the challenges associated with dating is different. The main concern I addressed with both of my children, was for them not to make short term goals, like dating, a priority over their life goals of graduating from high school, college, and pursuing their career. As much as I cringe internally sometimes when talking about dating with my daughter in particular, that was a HUGE proud poppa bear moment to hear she was making wise decisions about dating.

As my children transitioned from middle school to high school, I continued my ritual and routine of using meal time to establish open lines of communication. It was a break away from the routine of work and school and created a safe, calm, intimate environment where they could discuss and talk about things that were on their minds. Driving in the car was another place where we talked that was even less threatening, because we wouldn't be look-ing directly in each other's face while they were sharing. This made the liberty to talk less threatening for them. Talking in the car about their day, how they were feeling, and what was on their mind, was something I started when they were in elementary school.

Prior to my children entering middle school, I had set aside material for them to read on the subject of dating that a teenager had suggested I read. I would purchase copies of the books for high school teenagers because that was a major topic of discussion for them. It also showed how much they actually wanted to know and learn about the subject. My children were required to read the book, have open discussions with me and their mother, and wait until they were sixteen before they could have our permission to date.

QUESTIONS FOR PARENTS TO CONSIDER

1. What can parents do to help promote wisdom with their teenage child?

2. What are ways to help teenage children think critically?

3. Why is it important to not always tell your children what to do when they need to practice problem solving?

4. Why is it helpful to affirm, praise, and commend teenage children when they demonstrate wisdom in their decision making?

QUESTIONS FOR CHILDREN TO CONSIDER

1. Why is it important to not always rely on emotions when making decisions especially related to dating?

2. What can you do to demonstrate to your parents being a wise problem solver?

3. What does it mean to be a critical thinker and what do you think critical thinking requires?

4. Beyond high school why would decision making, problem solving, and critical thinking be important life skills to have?

STOP / THINK / PROCEED WITH CAUTION

What are your thoughts?

_____

_____

_____

_____

_____

_____

_____

_____

_____

_____

_____

_____

_____

_____

_____

CHAPTER 15

STRATEGIES FOR SUCCESS

The plans of the diligent lead to profit as surely as haste leads to poverty.

- Proverbs 21:5 NIV

WHY is it important for teenage children to learn life skills such as goal setting, time management, and strategic planning?

I actually had a conversation with a high school student who was upset with her mom because her mom was encouraging her to date when the student was content with being single. It bothered her that her mother wasn't accepting her choice to focus on doing well academically over the emphasis of dating. It led her mother to question her about her sexuality. The student took offense that her mother was so insistent about it, to the point of thinking something was wrong with her for not wanting to date. That conversation led me to consider whether or not there was insecurity on the part of the mother caused by her daughter's lack of interest in dating. When my daughter was born, the first thing I thought about, with great anxiety, was the reality that one day she would desire to date and have a boyfriend, lol. It is untrue to say children don't have any problems or anything to worry about. I have a colleague who co-facilitates parent seminars with me monthly. One thing she communicates consistently, related to middle school students in particular, is peer pressure being on steroids. She says this with regard to what youth are exposed to in today's culture, in comparison to the older generations.

I have explained to my children and students that asking for help is a life skill. Even as adults, we eventually find ourselves in circumstances that require us to ask for help, like getting driving directions when we're lost. Teaching writing enrichment on the middle school level, I actually teach my students life skills surrounding self-esteem, emotional literacy, critical thinking, problem solving, decision making, time management, demonstrating character, and learning to display an initiative mindset. An initiative mindset is consistently learning to do what needs to be done, without being told to. I explain that middle and high school students are at an age where they should not have to constantly be told to do what they know needs to be done, if they desire to be seen as responsible and mature while transitioning into adulthood.

Career exploration and career decision making as it relates to identifying coursework required in high school and college, along with identifying which colleges and universities have the best programs for their career interests, are important for our teenage children to learn to do. My daughter started her career path tracking in middle school, following the advice I gave her about identifying career interests and the career path needed to move towards her desired future. By her senior year in high school she could identify colleges of interest, their cost, and the coursework required to pursue her career interest in civil engineering. Her initial interest was in becoming an architect, and after taking her to an architectural firm to learn more, her interest changed to civil engineering. Exposing our teenagers to information and interests helps them to become effective decision makers over time.

QUESTIONS FOR PARENTS TO CONSIDER

1. What should a parent do if they're concerned about their child's social-emotional development?

2. What resources are accessible to parents to address any teen related concerns they might have about their child?

3. Why would the teenager's school counselor be a good place to start for a parent that has concerns about their teenager?

4. Why would the internet, or library, also be a good place to find information to address teen related concerns with your child?

QUESTIONS FOR CHILDREN TO CONSIDER

1. Why is it important to think critically about the future, goals, career interests, and how to get there? Why is it more important than dating?

2. What does it mean to focus more on what matters and less on what distracts?

3. What are some mistakes you have seen your peers make when they're dating, that hinders them from doing well at school?

4. Why is it dangerous to think that what a teenager sees happening to others in dating won't happen to them?

STOP / THINK / PROCEED WITH CAUTION

What are your thoughts?

_____

_____

_____

_____

_____

_____

_____

_____

_____

_____

_____

_____

_____

CHAPTER 16

CONCLUSION

When he came to his senses, he said, 'How many of my father's hired servants have food to spare, and here I am starving to death! I will set out and go back to my father and say to him: Father, I have sinned against heaven and against you.

- Luke 15:17-18 NIV

WHAT important life lessons, for parents and teens, are learned from the parable of the prodigal son?

There was a stretch of time spent with my children, now ages 19 and 17 respectively, where we would discuss the parable of the prodigal son. My main motivation in discussing this with them was to highlight an important life skill and principle essential to successful living. The son demanded he receive his inheritance, now, from his father. The father gave not only the inheritance to the son who asked for it, but also to the son who didn't. The son who demanded the inheritance then left home and squandered all he had in a lifestyle that consumed his resources. Then a famine came and he had to go and find employment. I explained to my children, the problem was him demanding something he should have waited until the time designated to receive, He also didn't have a plan in place on sustaining the wealth he had inherited. Due to his lack of foresight, the son squandered what was inherited instead of learning how to earn income, so when hard times came, he could have preserved his wealth. I wanted my children to understand the importance of learning to wait for those short-term things they desired, like dating, and learn to invest in things that mattered more so they could be better prepared for where they desire to go in the future.

The obvious problem of the parable, is the impetuous behavior of the son and his disregard for his father, by demanding an inheritance he was designated to receive upon his father's death. I would remind my children to avoid the attitude of demanding now what they need to learn to wait patiently for. However, teenagers have a tendency to demand things like sex, dating, driving, partying, money, but are most likely not demonstrating the wisdom, character, and maturity to acquire what they desire.

As I have explained to my son, most parents who love their children, are not going to willingly give their children permission to date, understanding that the grave challenges associated with it can ultimately lower the trajectory of a child's launch into adulthood. In the parable, the father is a representation of God and His love for His children that allows Him to give them things even when they don't deserve it. He ultimately knows how His generosity His children understand His loving nature when they need Him most. Understanding the loving nature of his father, the son realizes the error of his ways, comes to his senses and sees the solution to his current problem is getting his father's help. Establishing open lines of communication becomes a lifelong life-line extended to our children. If we commit to learning to talk with them now, they'll continue to do so when they need us most.

STOP / THINK / PROCEED WITH CAUTION

What are your thoughts?

_____

_____

_____

_____

_____

_____

_____

_____

_____

_____

_____

_____

_____

_____

_____

CONTACT US

Testimonials

We want to hear from you. If you enjoyed the content of our books on teen dating: Isaiah's book for Teens and my Parent Edition, share a testimonial using my email info@cortlandjones.com or visit my website www.cortland-jones.com. Share your thoughts using the Contact Us link.

Please post or share an image (by email or social media) with us about the books and include the book in the image.

My Instagram username/handle is @cortlandjones

Your support is greatly appreciated!